Monument
to an
Iron Master

Written & Illustrated
By
Stuart Saint

www.Codnor.info

A Codnor & District Local History & Heritage
Publication.

Printed by George & Co Press, Langley Mill, Nottinghamshire and a special thank you to 'Jacksdale Area Culture & Heritage' (JACHs) and the 'Portland Path Project' for all their help with this publication.

The Jessop Monument was erected in A.D. 1854,
by the workmen and friends of the late
William Jessop, Esq., of Butterley Hall,
in this county, as a tribute to his private work,
great talents, and public excellence.
Born A.D., 1784, died A.D., 1852

Limited First Edition
2013

ISBN 978-0-9572416-1-9

Contents

Introduction

Jessop Monument 2012. Author's collection

Overlooking the Erewash valley on the northern most ridge of the ancient deer park of Codnor, can be seen a tall stone column rising above the tree line.

This is a monument, built by the Butterley Company in the middle of the 19th century as a tribute to William Jessop *the younger*, who for many years was a partner in the Butterley Company and son of William Jessop *senior,* one of the four co-founders.

William was a popular and talented man with a strong engineering background. His father (William *senior*) was at the forefront of the canal building mania in Britain. His grandfather, Josias had been Quarter Master of his Majesty's Dockyard in Devonport and later worked alongside John Smeaton on the Eddystone Lighthouse.

Very little has been written about William Jessop *the younger* and even less about the monument that was built in his name.
Some of the original Butterley Company records still exist in the Derbyshire Records Office, but a good many are missing or destroyed.

There are no documents in the Derbyshire archive, that appear to relate to the initial planning or building of the monument, which may explain why nobody has bothered to write about it in any length.

Having a keen interest in the local history of Codnor and Golden Valley I have attempted to remedy this historical omission, in my own small way, with this long overdue publication.

I have tried to collate as many fragments of information that still exist about the Jessop Monument in this short book before they are lost or forgotten.

Some primary sources of information are available in the form of maps and directories as well as newspaper articles and the personal experiences of local people, who can still remember visiting the monument grounds when they were open.

There is also reliable secondary information available in the individual works of Philip Riden and Dudley V Fowkes, who have both written detailed books and papers on the Butterley Company.

(Please see the bibliography at the end of this book).

A Brief History of The Butterley Company

The Butterley Company was one of the most prosperous companies in the Midlands during the late eighteen and early nineteen hundreds, providing employment for generations of workers for over two hundred years.

The origins of the Butterley Company started back in 1790 when two business partners, Benjamin Outram and Francis Beresford, purchased the Butterley Estate near Ripley in Derbyshire. Their intention was to exploit the rich coal and ironstone deposits in the area.

Together with other local coal owners, they supported a proposal to build a canal between Langley Mill and Cromford to transport coal and ironstone mined in the Erewash valley and also bring in limestone from Crich to use in their newly built ironworks near Ripley.

The partners were joined a year later by William Jessop who had been appointed principal engineer for the canal project and John Wright, a banker from Nottingham. This partnership became known as Benjamin Outram & Co. A few years later after Benjamin Outram's death in 1805 the Company was renamed as the Butterley Company.

This fledgling company spent its early years developing the canal system, building steam winding engines for mines and laying the foundations of the modern railway network. This investment in the transport infrastructure and also the building of a second ironworks in neighbouring Codnor Park meant that by 1830 the Butterley Company was able to supply over a third of Derbyshire's pig iron production and was the largest producer of coal in the East Midlands.

The Butterley Company became a major force in the iron industry, the two ironworks producing rails and wagons for the railways, steam engines and boilers for use in mines and steam navigation and iron girders and cranes for some of the biggest civil engineering projects in the country.
Probably the most famous of these early engineering feats has to be the roof of St. Pancras Station in London, built in 1868. This single 240ft span of glass and cast iron framework was the largest structure of its kind in the world.

The Butterley Company also established brick works at Ollerton and Waingroves, producing bricks to erect factories and domestic dwellings.
New communities sprang up at Hammersmith and Golden Valley where rows of new houses were built. The first half of the 19th century also saw the creation of Ironville, a model village built by the Butterley Company to house workers for the Codnor Park Ironworks and local collieries.

*Construction of St. Pancras Station, London 1868 . This picture shows
Butterley company iron beams arriving by rail from Codnor Park Ironworks.
Authors collection*

The Butterley Company lost all of its mining interests during the
nationalisation of the coal industry in 1946. They still continued with their civil
engineering and brick making, but also diversified into farming.

The Butterley Company farms ran profitably into the 1950's until opencast
mining operations led to the abandonment of large-scale farming.

By the 1960's the Butterley Company was in its twilight years, the Codnor Park
Ironworks closed in 1965 and this was followed shortly afterwards by the sale
of the remaining Butterley works to Lord Hanson for £4.7 million.
The company was subsequently split up into Butterley Engineering (Ripley),
Butterley Brick (Waingroves) and Butterley Aggregates (Lincoln).

The early 1990's saw a slump in the building industry resulting in the closure
of the brickworks in Waingroves.

The engineering works at Ripley continued doing what they did best, building
bridges, cranes and structural steel work, but by 2009 the Butterley Company
succumbed to the economic downturn and went into administration on 5th
March 2009. Demolition of the works commenced later the same year and now
only the oldest listed buildings remain intact.

However before the end came, the Butterley Company was able to complete two final engineering projects. The first was the Falkirk Wheel, which opened in 2002. This is a rotating boatlift connecting the Forth & Clyde Canal with the Union Canal in Scotland and it replaced eleven locks. The lift is so well balanced that despite its combined carrying capacity of 600 tonnes it uses only 22.5kw of electricity to rotate 180° in just five minutes.

The final great engineering project was the manufacture of the steelwork for the Spinnaker tower, which stands 560ft high in Portsmouth harbour. The steel arcs, which form part of the structure, are designed to look like a billowing sail on a ship. The Spinnaker Tower is the tallest accessible building in England outside London.

Although the Butterley Company's specialist business activities left it vulnerable during the 2008 recession, it will always be remembered locally as the ironworks that emerged from the Industrial Revolution and went on to become a great engineering company, responsible for constructing some of the most ambitious engineering projects in the world.
The Falkirk wheel and Spinnaker Tower are testament to this and I'm sure if Outram, Wright, Beresford and Jessop could see these two incredible structures today they would be very proud indeed.

William Jessop *the younger*

William Jessop *the younger* was born in Fairburn, North Yorkshire sometime during the early part of the year 1784. His mother was Sarah Sawyer and she had married William's father, William Jessop *Senior*, in 1777.
Shortly after William's birth the family moved to a house in Appletongate, Newark, Nottinghamshire.

William had six brothers and a sister, the eldest was John who served in the army between 1798 an 1815. He was a Major in the 44th Regiment serving under The Duke of Wellington at Waterloo.
He was severely wounded by cannon fire at Quatre Bras, after which he was awarded the Waterloo medal and The Most Honourable Order of the Bath, Companion (C.B).
When he retired from the army he lived out the rest of his life as a country gentleman at Butterley Hall.

Next was Josias who was a brilliant engineer. He initially worked with his father, gaining engineering experience before going on to head projects such as the building of the Lydney Canal and the Wey and Arun Junction Canal. He was also appointed consultant engineer for the Cromford & High Peak Railway but died before the line was completed.

William's younger brother Charles joined the Navy in 1799 at the age of 13 as a first class volunteer.
He had the ambition of becoming an officer, but in October the same year he lost his life on HMS *Lutine* when it sank in a storm between the islands of Vlieland and Terschelling just off the Dutch coast.

The vessel was bound for Hamburg with a substantial cargo of gold and silver, which also went down with the ship.
Despite dozens of salvage attempts over the years, only a fraction of the valuable cargo has ever been recovered.

The ship's bell was found and it now hangs in the Lloyds Building in London.

The next brother was Henry who also trained as an engineer. He went over to India in 1818 to erect a Butterley Company iron bridge, over the Gomptee River. Whilst in India he established an engineering company called Jessop &

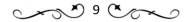

Co. This company was taken over by the Indian Government in 1973 and is now part of the Ruia Group and is the oldest engineering company in India.

The next brother was George and he was also involved in the running of Jessop & Co. He remained a partner in the business until his wife's death in 1834, when he retired shortly afterwards, and returned to England.

William's only sister, Sarah married Hugh Scott Esq. of Draycott on 14th September 1814 at Pentrich church, Derbyshire.
He was commander of the East India Company's ship, *Ceres*. They had no children.

The last brother Edward died at the relatively young age of 31 in Neilgherry Hills, India were he had been working as an assistant Surgeon.

William Jessop *Senior* had expected his eldest son, John to take over as a partner in the Butterley Company after his death, but John was not interested in the family business and he renounced the right in his father's Will to succeed into the partnership.

In his place it was young William, who become involved in the day-to-day running of the Butterley Company under the supervision of his father.
In 1805 shortly after William started working with the company, Benjamin Outram died leaving Butterley Hall vacant. The Jessop's left their home in Newark and moved into the Hall to be close to the Ripley Works.

Jessop Family Tree

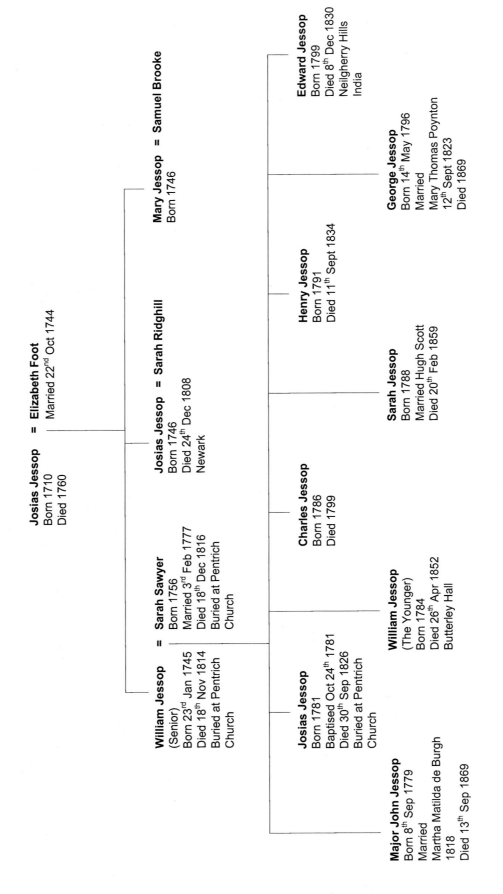

Josias Jessop
Born 1710
Died 1760

=

Elizabeth Foot
Married 22nd Oct 1744

William Jessop
(Senior)
Born 23rd Jan 1745
Died 18th Nov 1814
Buried at Pentrich
Church

=

Sarah Sawyer
Born 1756
Married 3rd Feb 1777
Died 18th Dec 1816
Buried at Pentrich
Church

Josias Jessop **=** **Sarah Ridghill**
Born 1746
Died 24th Dec 1808
Newark

Mary Jessop **=** **Samuel Brooke**
Born 1746

Josias Jessop
Born 1781
Baptised Oct 24th 1781
Died 30th Sep 1826
Buried at Pentrich
Church

William Jessop
(The Younger)
Born 1784
Died 26th Apr 1852
Butterley Hall

Charles Jessop
Born 1786
Died 1799

Sarah Jessop
Born 1788
Married Hugh Scott
Died 20th Feb 1859

Henry Jessop
Born 1791
Died 11th Sept 1834

George Jessop
Born 14th May 1796
Married
Mary Thomas Poynton
12th Sept 1823
Died 1869

Edward Jessop
Born 1799
Died 8th Dec 1830
Neilgherry Hills
India

Major John Jessop
Born 8th Sep 1779
Married
Martha Matilda de Burgh
1818
Died 13th Sep 1869

After his father's death in 1814, William would have looked to the loyal support of the works manager Mr George Goodwin to assist him.

William had the passion and ability to continue were his father had left off and in 1815 he signed an agreement with the remaining partner, John Wright and became co-owner of the Butterley Company.

However, when William signed the agreement he could not have expected this new role in the company to put his very life in danger.

Just two weeks after William became a partner, Napoleon was defeated at Waterloo and the long running Napoleonic wars came to an end, but this left Britain in deep depression.

Mass unemployment following the demobilisation of the armed forces and increased mechanisation of industry meant the average working man struggled to earn a living. Poor crops and unfair taxes to recover the war debt made the situation even worse.

All over the country could be heard mutterings of discontent. Groups of men gathered in barns and back rooms of public houses and talk of revolution was in the air.

One such meeting was held on 5th June 1817 in the White Horse public house in Pentrich. Jeramiah Brandreth, an unemployed Stockinger from Sutton-in-Ashfield, planned to lead a group of revolutionaries on a march to Nottingham to join ranks with other groups from the North.

Their intention was then to march to London and overthrow the government. The first part of the plan was to take control of the Butterley Ironworks at Ripley. They were to kill the owner, William Jessop and the two work's managers, Mr Goodwin, and Mr Wragg then retrieve any arms that could be found there and force the workers to join their ranks.

What they didn't know at the time was that there would be no other groups to meet them at Nottingham, in fact they had a spy in their midst, an *agent provocateur* named William Oliver. Evidence suggests that he was working for Lord Sidmouth, the Home Secretary and that he had informed the authorities of the potential uprising.

On June 9th 1817 the plan was put into action. Jeramiah Brandreth together with William Turner and Isaac Ludlam gathered a small group of men at South Wingfield and headed towards the Butterley Ironworks, increasing their numbers on the way by press ganging men to join them from local farms and villages. Any who refused were threatened with violence and one farm servant was shot dead by Brandreth when he refused to open the door to the mob.

By the time they got to the ironworks they were about a hundred strong and armed with pitchforks, pikes and some farm shotguns, but William Jessop had already been made aware of their intentions.

Jessop and Goodwin, together with a small group of constables who had been 'sworn in' the previous day, were waiting for them.
When Brandreth and his men arrived at the works, the gates were locked and Mr Goodwin refused them entry. Brandreth demanded men and arms, but Mr Goodwin would let him have none.

Frustrated by this setback and unwilling to confront the armed constables, Brandreth marched his men off through Ripley and Codnor eventually reaching just the other side of Eastwood before they were intercepted by mounted troops from the local barracks.

A total of thirty-five men were charged with high treason at a trial in Derby. Brandreth, Turner and Ludlum were sentenced to be hung drawn and quartered, but this was commuted to hanging then beheading; many of the other convicted rioters were transported to Australia.

Brandreth, Turner and Ludlum paid a high price for their role in the Pentrich uprising.

The Butterley company soon began to prosper under the partnership of Jessop and Wright and they won many high profile engineering contracts including the building of the Vauxhall Bridge over the river Thames and also supplying the rails and winding engines for the Cromford and High Peak Railway.

In 1824, William Jessop purchased the coal and minerals within the old Marquis of Ormonde estate at Codnor for 7000 guineas. This allowed the Butterley Company to expand their mining activities south through Codnor and Loscoe towards Heanor.

None of this expansion would have been possible without the Company's investment in the many horse drawn tramways that conveyed coal and ironstone to the wharves on the Cromford canal built by William Jessop's father in the 1790's.

This combination of tramways and waterways enabled the company to transport coal south, down the Erewash canal and Soar navigation into Leicestershire. This efficient transport network meant that Derbyshire coal could be sold in Leicester, far cheaper than the Leicestershire coal owners could achieve. They had no choice but to transport their coal by road using horse and cart, which left them at a great disadvantage.

However, by 1830 a new railway between Leicester and Swannington had been approved, which would provide the Leicestershire coalfields with the transportation link they had previously lacked.
George Stephenson and his son Robert were the engineers asked to oversee the new project. Jessop recognised that any such railway, if successful could seriously affect the Butterley Company's monopoly on coal sales in Leicestershire.

So on the 17th July 1832 William Jessop, representing the Butterley Company and James Oakes, representing James Oakes & Co, together with several Erewash Canal directors attended the grand opening of the Leicester and Swannington Railway to judge for themselves how effective the new railway was likely to be.

The railway was opened by a train of open carriages decorated with banners advertising "Cheap Coal and Granite" and carrying hundreds of officials and a brass band. It was drawn by a new steam engine called the "Comet" built by Messr's Robert Stephenson & Co and driven by George Stephenson himself.

Unfortunately for Jessop and the rest of the Erewash contingent, the opening run of the Leicester and Swanninton line was a huge success and proved beyond doubt that it would be more than capable of transporting coal from the Leicestershire coal fields rather than relying on shipping coal down the Erewash canal from Derbyshire.

The only cheerful thought that Jessop could take away from the day's events was the memory of Comet's chimney being dislodged as it passed through the Glenfield tunnel and the sudden transformation of the appearance of the passengers as the train emerged from the other side, the combination of steam and smoke having coated the ladies and gentlemen with a layer of greasy black soot.

Ironically the new train ran on edge rails of "fish-belly" construction, a design pioneered by William Jessop's father during his early years working for the Butterley Company. These later edge rails were an improvement over the earlier cast iron plate rails favoured by Benjamin Outram and made it possible for heavier, faster, steam locomotives such as Stephenson's *Comet* to be developed.

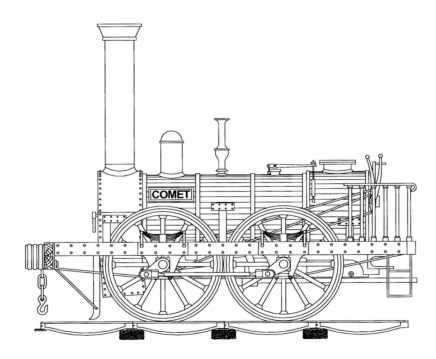

Jessop recognised that the combination of the newly opened Leicester and Swannington Railway and Stephenson's Comet locomotive, would pose a serious threat to the Butterley Company's coal sales in Leicestershire.

Jessop reported the success of the Leicester and Swanninton line back to the Derbyshire and Nottinghamshire coal owners and stated that if they intended to compete with this railway they would need to reduce their price of coal sold in Leicestershire by *3s 6d* per ton.

The coal owners agreed to drop their coal price by 1s per ton if the canal companies would reduce their rates by 3s. But the canal companies said they would lose too much money and only agreed to reduce their rates by 1s 6d. It was obvious an agreement could not be reached with the canal companies' and so on the 16th August 1832 a meeting of the Derbyshire Coal owners was held at the Sun Inn Eastwood where they rejected the offer from the canal companies and instead unanimously agreed to build their own railway.

"There remains no other plan for our adoption than to attempt to lay a railway from these collieries to the town of Leicester".

A committee was elected and the Sun Inn became the birthplace of the Midland Counties Railway Company. William Jessop was on the board of directors and was responsible for the initial survey for the intended line in 1832. It was re-surveyed by George Rennie who confirmed Jessop's results, however the investors who were known as the 'Liverpool party' were not happy with the proposed route and required that any new line should form a link in the chain of railways between London and the North.

So yet another engineer by the name of Charles Blacker Vignoles was asked for an alternative survey that would link Rugby to Derby via Leicester with a branch line to Nottingham.
The new survey was passed and the line opened in three stages:-

Derby to Nottingham 4th June 1839,
Trent Junction to Leicester 4th May 1840
Leicester to Rugby 1st July 1840.

Jessop had to wait a further seven years before he eventually got a railway line to his collieries and Ironworks at Codnor park in the form of the Erewash Valley Railway opened on 6th September 1847.

The Midland Counties Railway eventually evolved into the Midland Railway Company, taking over the Erewash Valley Railway and the Leicester and Swanninton railway in the process.

William Jessop always preferred to be known as an "Iron Master" rather than an Engineer. Maybe he lived in the shadow of his father, who's great engineering achievements were at the forefront of the industrial revolution in Britain.

Nevertheless William was still a brilliant engineer and the Butterley Company benefited from many of his ideas and inventions, giving them an advantage over their competitors.

For example he patented a mechanism for accurately loading proportions of ironstone and limestone into the Butterley blast furnaces, equally distributing the mixture inside. This process produced a high quality cast iron that was much sought after.

He also patented a design of piston to be used in steam engines. It was called the 'Elastic Metallic Piston' and incorporated a packing of helical coil steel, which could be adjusted to compensate for any wear between the piston and cylinder.

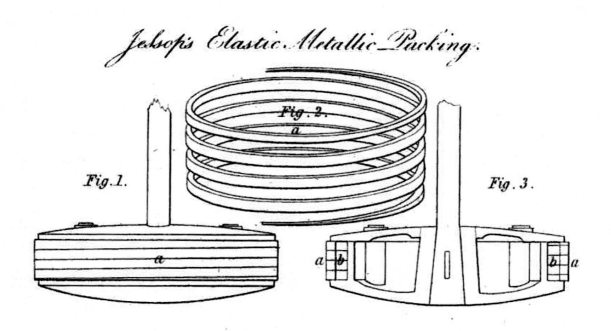

Jessop's Elastic Metallic Piston. Patent No.4770 March 27th 1823

Authors collection.

He also developed a style of rail chair designed to compensate for any displacement of the railway sleepers on soft ground without affecting the alignment of the rails themselves.

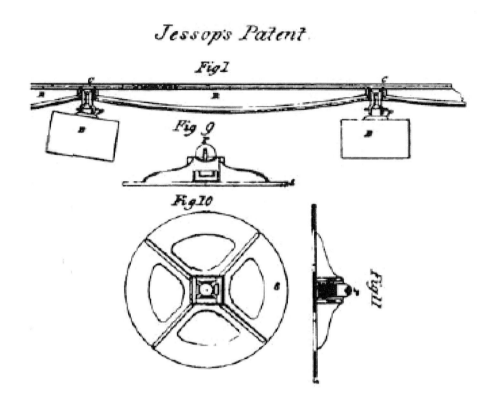

Improvements in constructing railways, Patent No. 6433 June 1st 1833
Authors collection

William Jessop the younger was popular with his workforce and always took their social needs into consideration. During his years as a partner he had organised the Ripley and Pentrich Volunteers, Butterley's defence against a French Invasion, built schools and chapels in the local communities and provided secure employment and homes for a majority of the local population.

He never married; but instead devoted his entire working life to the development of the Butterley Company that his father had co-founded. In his spare time he enjoyed breeding dogs, which he entered in Hare Coursing events. One of his dogs was named *Jos* after his brother Josias.

By the time William retired in 1851 the company was heading into the most prosperous era in its history, but William never got to see this. He suffered a long illness after his retirement and died a year later at Butterley Hall on 26th April 1852.

Newcastle Journal Saturday 1st May 1852

Deceased *At Butterley Hall, Derbyshire, on the 26th ult. William Jessop, Esq. Mr Jessop had retired from business in consequence of the infirmities of increasing years, some time ago, and gradually declined, till he closed his account on earth on the evening of the above-named day, after a long life of probably the most active character ever sustained by a man of business. He was, in earlier life, the associate of the first engineers of the day, and with them was instrumental in maturing as well as projecting many of the great and useful engineering works of that day; projects that astonished men then, and were the foundations that prepared the way for those wonders that astonish the world now. He has left many monuments of his talents behind him, and many friends and dependents who universally mourn his loss. Mr Jessop was one of the partners in the iron house known as the "Butterley Company."*

A French Industrialist once wrote the following paragraph to a friend, after learning of William's death.

"The Butterley Company has lost her governor and the workmen their father. I read in many of our works in metallurgy that Mr Jessop was one of the most learned Ironmasters in England. May he have a just reward for the good he has done to his workmen and to society".

The east window in Christ church, Ironville was also erected as a memorial to his memory and the inscription reads as follows;

These windows were erected in memory of William JESSOP, who died April 26th Anno Domini 1852.

The Monument

After William Jessop's death in 1852, the Butterley Company decided that some kind of memorial or better still a monument was required, as a lasting tribute to his life's work.

A seven-acre plot of land was chosen at the northern end of Codnor park, just before the land started to slope down towards Ironville to the North and the River Erewash to the East. The plot was ideal as it over-looked both the Butterley and Codnor Park Estates. This plot was also in dire need of a face-lift as it had been mined extensively by the Butterley Company's "Upper Park" pits for several decades and as a consequence was littered with abandoned spoil heaps. It had also been used for quarrying stone, so any improvements to what must have been quite an eyesore would have been most welcome.

In 1853 an appeal was made for subscriptions towards the building of such a monument and this was accompanied by the following tribute.

"To erect a monument to the late William Jessop, Esq.. Seems almost a work of supererogation as his own genius, energy, singleness of purpose, determination of character, perseverance and generosity of conduct have earned fame for himself and stamped a name and character upon the whole of the Erewash Valley that will never die; indeed his name as passed the limits of his own district, and not only there but of his own country".

A plan of the proposed monument was unveiled at a meeting at Codnor Park & Ironville School, but it wasn't to everybody's liking as the following newspaper article reveals:-

Nottinghamshire Guardian Thursday, December 15th, 1853
The Jessop Monument. – It is proposed to erect a monument to the late Mr. William Jessop, the well-known iron-master, of the Erewash Valley. The Butterley Company have granted a piece of land: a design has been obtained (how we do not hear), and subscriptions are being solicited.. If the rude lithograph in circulation shows the design determined on, the best we can give the committee is, that they may not succeed in getting money enough to execute it. It is a plain column full of loop holes, with a pedestal, capital, and termination, perfectly nondescript,- the whole 90 feet in height. It is a cross between a light-house and a factory chimney,- only worse. It is to be hoped that the committee will take proper advice before they waste the subscribers' money.- The Builder.

By Late 1853 the details had been agreed and work started on the monument site. A young boy out walking with his father was asked by the workers to turn the first sod to symbolise the start of the building project.

The boy's name was William Samuel Greaves and his father was Abraham Greaves, the local chemist from Ironville.

William Samuel Greaves *1843 – 1904*

A portrait of William Samuel Greaves extracted from the
St. Mary's, Westwood Diamond Jubilee Bazaar Programme 1897.
Displayed courtesy Martyn Taylor Cockayne.

William Samuel Greaves was born at number 49 King William Street, Ironville, which was also his father's chemist shop. He registered as a Chemist in 1864 and worked alongside his father in their shop, Greaves & Son. Abraham Greaves left the family business in the early 1870s and established Greaves & Richardson Chemist in Chesterfield. William took over the family business in Ironville and built a new shop "W.S.Greaves Limited" in Jacksdale. William Samuel Greaves died on 28th June 1904 at his home at Laurel Bank, Codnor Park.

The foundations for the monument were prepared during September 1854 and the first stone was laid by Mr Francis Wright, of Osmaston Manor on October 9th 1854 and construction continued for nearly three years.

Derby Mercury Wednesday 18th October 1854

The Monument To The Late W. Jessop, Esq.*-The first stone of the monument to be erected to the memory of the late W Jessop, Esq., managing partner of the Butterley Company, was laid on Monday, the 9th inst., By F.Wright, Esq., W.Needham, Esq., J.Radford, Esq., Mr Barber, the Rev. Gerard Smith, the Rev. J.Casson, Mr Smith (the oldest servant of the company), Mr College, and the Rev. E. Davies, assisted at the ceremonial. A long procession of the workmen of the Butterley Company was formed from the different works, headed by the Selston and Codnor Park brass band. A number of flags with suitable inscriptions were carried by the senior workmen. A beautiful silver trowel, manufactured by Messrs. Wales and Mc'Cullock, London, was subscribed for by the ladies of Ironville and Codnor Park, which was beautifully engraved with the following;-*

"Presented to F. Wright, Esq., by the ladies of Ironville, on the occasion of his laying the first stone of the Jessop Monument, September, 1854."

A public tea was afterwards provided in the school-rooms at Ironville, kindly granted for the occasion by the Butterley Company, at the close of which the party present were addressed by F. Wright, Esq., and other gentlemen. Throughout the day the village had the appearance of a holiday, all the shops being closed at 1pm.

When the building was completed the gritstone monument consisted of a square pedestal mounted by a round column of ashler blocks reaching a height somewhere between 70 and 90 feet (documents from the period give conflicting information).

This was then topped off by a square cast iron viewing platform, which was reached by an internal spiral staircase of 150 stone steps.
The total cost of building the monument was £700, which was raised by public subscriptions.

On the North facing side of the plinth, a stone tablet was mounted with the following inscription.

This Monument was erected

In A.D. 1854,

by the workmen and friends

of the late

William Jessop, Esq.,

of Butterley Hall,

in this county,

as a tribute to

his private work,

great talents,

and public excellence.

Born A.D., 1784, died A.D., 1852

When the Monument grounds were finally opened in 1857, one of the first events to be held there was the annual festival of the "Codnor Park & Ironville Artisans & Mechanics Library" this had previously been held in the grounds of Codnor Castle, just half a mile to the south and was always popular and well attended.

So in August that year they held their 14th annual festival in the Jessop Monument grounds for the very first time.

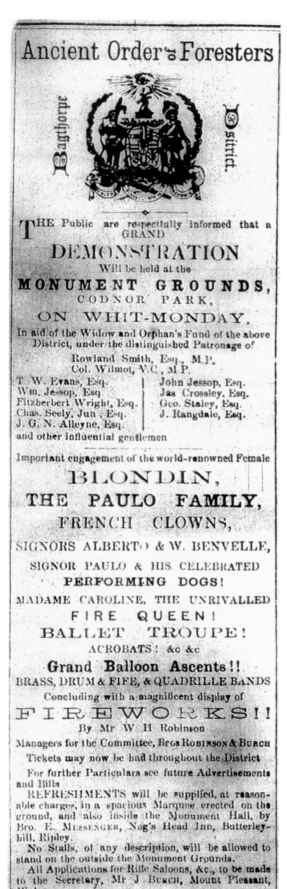

Advertisement for Whit Monday 1869

GRAND DEMONSTRATION AT THE MONUMENT GROUNDS

The advert lists the "World-renowned female Blondin". She was known as Madame Caroline, real name Caroline Prigg.

A few weeks after Madame Caroline's appearance at the Jessop Monument she was performing a tightrope walk between two buildings in Bolton. She slipped and was left dangling precariously above the crowd.

Eventually she had to let go of the rope and fell sixty feet into the arms of a group of men who had assembled below. Despite the distance that she fell, she suffered no injuries.

Caroline's husband was Henry John Butcher, who performed as part of "The Paulo family", also in the same advert.

Image displayed courtesy Martin Whyld

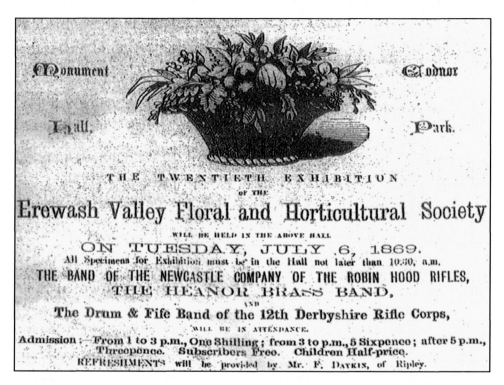

Twentieth Exhibition of the Erewash Valley Floral and Horticultural Society Tuesday July 6th 1869. The show of flowers, Fruits and vegetables was not as large as on previous occasions due to the poor season.
Image displayed courtesy Martin Whyld.

Some other examples of events include:

Permissive Bill Demonstration, Whit Monday 6th June 1870

The Ripley and Riddings Temperance Societies held a grand temperance *fete* on the Monument Grounds, Codnor Park, on Monday, when there was a very large gathering. Deputations from the United Kingdom Alliance and British Temperance League had representatives present to deliver addresses. Also attending were the Rev. W.E.Littlewood, vicar of Ironville, Mr Alfred Smedley of Belper (Chairman) and Mr J Birch, the converted negro player, who sang some of his popular melodies. Bands included The 12th Derbyshire Rifle Corps Drum & Fife Band, The Ruddington Temperance Brass Band and the Codnor Quadrille Band. There was bicycle racing and other amusements, refreshments were provided by Mr Daykin of Ripley.

Grand Fete and Gala, Monday 14th April 1873

Organised by W.H.Robinson of Ripley, including Nottingham String Band, Heanor Brass Band and also a firework display. "A large company patronised the occasion".

Meeting

In the MONUMENT GROUNDS, CODNOR PARK, SATURDAY, JUNE 21st, 1919,
—— 4 p.m. ——

Speaker — MR. W. R. RAE
(SUNDERLAND).

MR. JOSEPH TINSLEY
(President of the Society) in the Chair.

□ □ □

Resolution.

Proposer — MR. R. HANSON.
Seconder — MR. J. DEXTER.

THAT this Meeting, whilst rejoicing over the progress of our Society during the last 50 years, and the many benefits consequently accruing to its members, past and present, heartily congratulates the Codnor Park & Ironville Equitable Industrial Co-operative Society Limited on the attainment of its Jubilee, and desires to record its warm appreciation of the services rendered by Committees, Officials and Employees, past and present, during the long period. It also urges upon all members the necessity of increasing their support of the Society, so that the manifold advantages of Co-operation, both Distributive and Productive may be still further extended.

An advert for the Golden Jubilee celebrations of the Codnor Park & Ironville Equitable Industrial Co-operative Society at the Monument Grounds 21st June 1919.

Image displayed courtesy Martyn Taylor Cockayne

This postcard from 1904 shows the lodge house at the entrance to the monument grounds, off monument lane. Author's collection

This hand coloured postcard from 1910 shows a large gathering of people enjoying a summer festival at the Jessop Monument. Author's collection

Probably the most popular event at the Jessop monument was the annual Whit Monday parade and festival.

Churches from all the surrounding villages were represented by children from the local Sunday schools, who paraded through the streets carrying flags and banners, some bearing temperance slogans such as "Wine is a Mocker" and "Strong Drink Is Raging". There would be girls dressed in white carrying the Maypole and also carts and drays decorated with flowers. These "Band of Hope" processions were led by the local village or colliery brass bands, who played rousing hymns as they marched out of the villages towards the monument.

Children from Wood Street Chapel, Ripley preparing to join the Band of Hope parade in 1920.
Image displayed courtesy Paul Birks

Once inside the monument grounds the girls would dance around the maypole and the bands would play a few more hymns on a stage erected at the side of the monument hall.

After this the children were free to do pretty much what they wanted for the rest of the day.

Fairground rides and swings were always popular with the children as was the Punch-and-Judy shows and the Aunt Sally stall.

Inside the monument hall would be exhibitions of drawings, needlework, and flower arranging with prizes being awarded for the best.

Refreshments of tea, cherryade, cakes and buns were also available throughout the day.

The Whit Monday festivals were probably at their most popular after the First World War. The events had to stop at the outbreak of the Second World War, when the hall was used by the Home Guard and Fire Watchers.

After the war the monument hall was converted into a Rola-Rena and sports hall with badminton courts marked out on the floor. However, access to the top of the monument was no longer possible, the temporary repairs undertaken in the 1860s were now considered unsafe and the monument was closed to public access once again.

By the late 1950s early 60s the days of the Codnor Park Monument festivals had long gone. Advances in public transport made access to modern venues further afield far more available to all and before long the grounds closed to visitors altogether.

The door to the Jessop Monument was bricked up and the hall locked and abandoned to the elements. Hawthorn bushes and nettles swallowing up the beautiful gardens and for the first time in over one hundred years, the monument and grounds lay empty and silent.

The Butterley Company sold the Codnor Park Estate, together with the Jessop Monument and grounds to Mr Bernard Swain in 1968. Mr Swain lived at Ormonde Fields House, Codnor, (now the Ormonde Fields Golf Club). Aspiring to live the life of a country gentleman he obtaining a Swain family coat of arms, which was granted by the Ulster Kings of Arms in 1970. He also kept fox hounds and would occasionally arrange fox hunting on the Codnor Park estate.

Mr Swain leased Jessop Monument lodge to his gamekeeper who used the monument hall to store fencing materials and pheasant pens.

Mr Swain sold the Codnor Park estate in 1978 and ownership of the Jessop Monument and grounds were transferred to the National Coal Board, who continued to treat it as private property and closed to public access.

This decision proved unpopular with the local people, who wrongly believed that there had always been public access on the roads around the monument. In fact access had only ever been 'by permission only'. The Butterley Company permitted the general public, free pedestrian access on all roads past the Jessop Monument on the basis that a majority of the local population already worked for the Butterley Company and used the roads daily to walk back and forth to their various places of work.

Mr Swain had no such obligations and was quick to close off the roads on the estate. The Coal Board followed suit during their period of ownership and the roads to the monument remained for private use only.

The decades passed by and the monument and hall fell into disrepair, the monument had been classed as a Grade Two listed building since 1966 and was later added to the English Heritage 'Buildings at Risk Register' as it was considered at risk of collapse unless structural repairs were urgently undertaken.

However, the money needed to finance the project was not forthcoming and it seemed likely that the Jessop monument's days were numbered.

A view from the top of the Jessop Monument looking over the fields towards Golden Valley and Newlands Farm, late 1980s. Authors collection.

Monument Restoration

By the early 1990s the Jessop Monument and hall were still standing, but in a decrepit state. However, a glimmer of hope came in 1993 when an application was put forward by British Coal (National Coal Board) for an opencast coal mine on land adjacent to the Jessop monument.

This initial application was rejected by Derbyshire County Council, who believed it offered little back to the local communities once the opencast mining was completed.

By 1996 British Coal mining activities had merged with RJB Mining to form UK Coal Plc. and they submitted a revised application to Derbyshire County Council. This application now included a Section 106 agreement, which required UK Coal to perform stabilisation repairs to both the Jessop Monument and hall and nearby Codnor Castle on completion of any opencast mining activities.

After a few more revisions the new application was accepted on the 24th August 1998 and a total of £1.5 million was allocated to pay for consolidation and repairs to both the historic buildings.

The opencast operations eventually got underway in 2001 and completed in 2004 but it would be another two years before restoration work was allowed to commence on the Jessop Monument. The work was carried out for UK Coal by Croft Building & Conservation Ltd from Cannock, a company who specialised in restoration work on historical buildings. Consolidation and repairs to both the Jessop Monument and Codnor Castle were completed by May 2008.

Remains of Codnor Castle in 1982, before it also received the much needed consolidation work, which was supervised by English Heritage.
Authors collection

The Jessop Monument 2006.
Displayed courtesy of Tamworth Scaffolding Company Limited

The amount of restoration work required on the monument was quiet extensive
and scaffolding had to be erected to allow access to the entire structure.
The cast iron platform was reinforced using stainless steel plates and missing
stones had to be replaced with new blocks.
Last of all a new lightning conductor was fitted.

.

Close up of the column showing the severity of the lightning strike. Displayed courtesy of Croft Building & Conservation Ltd.

The column after being restored with new Ashlar blocks cut on site. Displayed courtesy of Jon Howard

The viewing platform during restoration. The floor has been removed revealing details of the iron castings and spiral stone staircase.
Displayed courtesy of Croft Building & Conservation Ltd.

When the floor of the viewing platform was removed in 2006, a small two-inch long artefact was found in a hole in the top step. It is a barrel shaped pot engraved with the date 1857. It could have been placed there during a topping out ceremony on completion of the monument in 1857.
Displayed courtesy of Lesley Thraves

Interior of the monument hall before restoration, 1980s. The wooden floor was in poor condition in the 1950s when it was used as a Rola-Rena. Many older residents remember having to skate around the holes. Author's collection

The monument hall with restored copingstones and new cast iron gutters and down pipes to match the originals. The roof is new but only considered temporary. Author's collection

The Jessop Monument photographed in 2008 after completion of the restoration work. Author's collection

The first phase of the restoration work on the Jessop Monument and hall was completed in 2007, enabling both buildings to be removed from the English Heritage Buildings at Risk Register on the 1st September the same year, the second phase was completed in 2008.

The reason for the repairs and stabilisation was to preserve and protect the fabric of the buildings for future generations to enjoy. At the time of writing this book it was unclear what the long-term future had in store for the Jessop Monument.

A group of enthusiasts had previously set up The Jessop Monument Trust in 2003 to re-establish public access to the site and promote a programme of full and ongoing restoration, but they had found progress difficult.

In November 2007 an article in the Ripley and Heanor newspaper quotes a UK Coal spokesman as saying; "We are keen it should be used by the community – a discussion will take place between UK Coal, the county council, parish council and other groups to decide on its future". By 2010 no satisfactory decision regarding the monuments future had been reached and UK Coal advertised the site for sale.

Despite the Jessop Monument being originally paid for by public subscription, it is now private property and public access is not permitted.

For the time being at least the monument is safe, but it would be a shame if public access were denied on a permanent basis. Wouldn't it be nice if sometime in the future, some organised events could be held in the monument grounds? Such events could help pay for the ongoing maintenance required for this listed building or the reinstatement of a new plaque to replace the original that was destroyed.

Most of all it would give members of the public the opportunity to enjoy the hospitality of the Jessop Monument once again.

Acknowledgments

I would like to thank the following groups and individuals for their contributions to this publication.

Croft Building & Conservation Ltd, who provided information on the works carried out on the monument and hall, also for contributing the images on pages 44 & 45.

Tamworth Scaffolding Company Limited for contributing the image on page 43

Lesley Thraves for contributing the image on page 45

Martin Whyld for his contribution of historical material including the images on pages 34 and 35

Jon Howard for contributing the image on page 44

Paul Birks for contributing the images on pages 27 & 38

Carol and Martyn Taylor Cockayne for their contribution of historical material including the images on pages 21 & 36

Bibliography

1851 UK Census

Days In Derbyshire
by Dr. Spencer T Hall 1863, ISBN: 978-1246998450

Derby Mercury 17th July 1861

Derby Mercury 6th July 1864

Derby Mercury 12th August 1857

Map of Codnor Park 1722, Derbyshire Records office D769B/12/5/2

George Jessop Letters, Ref: D4753 Derbyshire Records Office

Illustrated London News 27th July 1861

Memoirs of William Jessop by Samuel Hughes: Weale's Quarterly Papers on Engineering 1844

Monument Day: by H.L.Burt 1998

My village: Owd Codnor by Joseph Millott Severn 1935 ASIN: B00087SW28

Newcastle Journal 1st May 1852

Nottinghamshire Guardian 15th December 1853

Nottinghamshire Guardian 25th July 1861

St. Mary's, Westwood Diamond Jubilee Bazaar Programme 1897

The Asiatic journal and monthly register for British and foreign India, China and Australasia, Volume 2 1830

The Butterley Company, 1790-1830
by Philip Riden ISBN: 978-0946324125

The Development Of Ironville: by Dudley V Fowkes

The History of the Midland Railway
by Clement Edwin Stretton 1901 ISBN: 978-1142078058

The London Gazette 10th December 1998

The London Gazette 4th August 1999

The Parish Registers of Ledsham in the county of York 1539 - 1812

The Ripley Advertiser 10th July 1866

The Ripley & Heanor News 28th May 1965

The Ripley & Heanor News 11th October 2001

The Ripley & Heanor News 14th August 2003

The Ripley & Heanor News 29th November 2007

The Trials of Jeremiah Brandreth, William Turner, Isaac Ludlam, George Weight.
by William Brodie Gurney 1817   ISBN: 978-1147171778

Through five generations: The history of the Butterley Company
by R. H Mottram and Colin Coote 1950

William Jessop, Engineer
by Charles Hadfield and A.W. Skempton ISBN: 978-0715376034